This Is a Let's-Read-and-Find-Out Science Book®

How We Learned the Earth Is Round

BY PATRICIA LAUBER
ILLUSTRATED BY MEGAN LLOYD

Thomas Y. Crowell   New York

The *Let's-Read-and-Find-Out Science Book* series was originated by Dr. Franklyn M. Branley, Astronomer Emeritus and former Chairman of the American Museum–Hayden Planetarium, and was formerly co-edited by him and Dr. Roma Gans, Professor Emeritus of Childhood Education, Teachers College, Columbia University. For a complete catalog of Let's-Read-and-Find-Out Science Books, write to Thomas Y. Crowell Junior Books, Harper & Row, Publishers, Inc., 10 East 53rd Street, New York, NY 10022.

Let's-Read-and-Find-Out Science Book is a registered trademark of Harper & Row, Publishers, Inc.

Photographs on pages 30, 31, and 32 appear courtesy of NASA.

Library of Congress Cataloging-in-Publication Data
Lauber, Patricia.
    How we learned the earth is round / by Patricia Lauber ;
illustrated by Megan Lloyd.
        p.   cm. — (Let's-read-and-find-out science book)
    Summary: Explains various changes in humanity's beliefs about the shape of the earth, from the flat earth theories of the ancients to the round earth theories that were proven true by the voyages of Columbus and Magellan.
    ISBN 0-690-04860-2 : $. — ISBN 0-690-04862-9 (lib. bdg.) : $
    1. Earth—Figure—Juvenile literature.   [1. Earth.]   I. Lloyd, Megan, ill.   II. Title.   III. Series.
QB286.L38   1990
525'.1—dc20
89-49650
CIP
AC

Stand out on the prairie.

Today nearly everybody knows that the earth is round.
But long ago, people were sure the earth was
flat. They thought it was flat because it looked flat.
It still does.

Climb a mountain. Now the earth looks rough and bumpy, but it doesn't seem to curve. It doesn't look round.

Sail out onto the ocean.
You can see for miles, and the earth looks flat.

The earth looks flat because it is big and we are small. We see only a tiny piece at one time. The tiny piece does curve, but the curve is too slight for our eyes to see. And that is why, for thousands of years, people thought the earth was flat.

The earth's real shape was discovered about 2,500 years ago. The people who discovered it were Greeks.

At first the Greeks, too, believed the earth was flat. But certain Greeks were great thinkers. They thought hard about things they saw and tried to explain them. They asked themselves questions—Why? What if? And then they thought some more.

Everybody knew that a strange thing happened when a ship left harbor. As it sailed away, it appeared to sink. First the hull disappeared, then the bottom of the sail, then the top.

As a ship returned, it seemed to rise out of the sea.
First the sail appeared, then the hull.
The Greeks wondered why.

Why didn't the whole ship just get smaller and smaller or bigger and bigger? That's what should happen on a flat earth.

But it didn't happen. Why didn't it?

Perhaps the answer had to do with the shape of the earth. Perhaps the earth wasn't flat after all. Perhaps it had some other shape.

What if the earth had a curved surface? What would happen to a ship then?

You can see what happens yourself. Use a big ball and a ship made from an eraser, a toothpick, and a piece of paper. With one hand, hold the ball in front of you at eye level. Use the other hand to move the ship.

When a ship sails away over a curved surface, the bottom disappears first. When it returns, the top appears first.

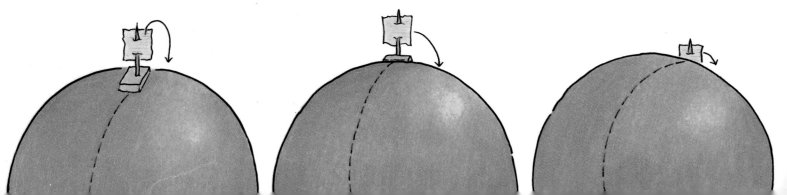

The Greeks decided the earth must have a curved surface. That would explain why ships seemed to sink and rise.

They also saw that the same thing happened no matter which way a ship was heading—east, west, north, or south. The earth must curve in all directions.

Was it round? They found the answer in the night sky.

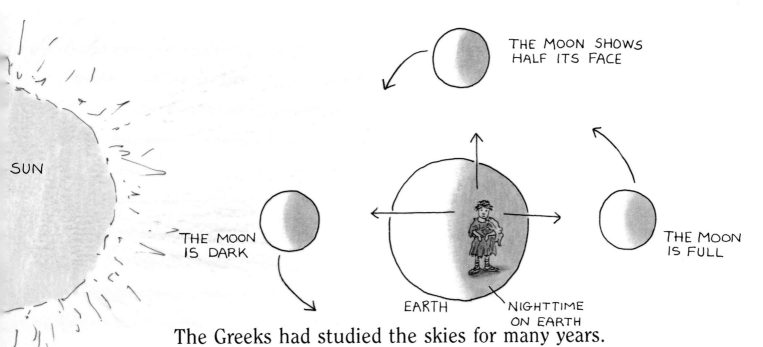

The Greeks had studied the skies for many years. They knew that the sun made its own light and the moon did not. The moon shone because it reflected light from the sun.

They also knew that the moon traveled around the earth. As it did so, different parts of it were lighted up by the sun. That was why the moon seemed to change its shape, why they might see a sliver of moon, a bigger piece, or a full moon. They saw a full moon whenever the moon was on the far side of the earth from the sun.

But sometimes a shadow dimmed the light of a full moon—an eclipse took place. The shadow seemed to sweep across the face of the moon. The edge of the shadow was curved. It was like part of a circle.

The Greeks knew that this shadow was the earth's. It was the shadow that the earth cast in space. When the moon moved through the shadow, an eclipse took place.

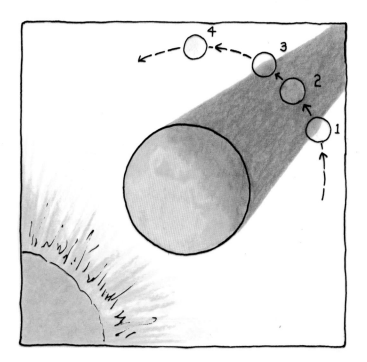

Sometimes the moon was high in the sky during an eclipse. Sometimes it was low. Yet as long as the sun, earth, and moon were lined up, an eclipse took place. And the edge of the shadow was always the same curve.

There is only one shape that always casts the same shadow. That shape is round. A ball, for example, always casts the same shadow no matter how it is turned. It casts the same shadow no matter where the light is coming from.

15

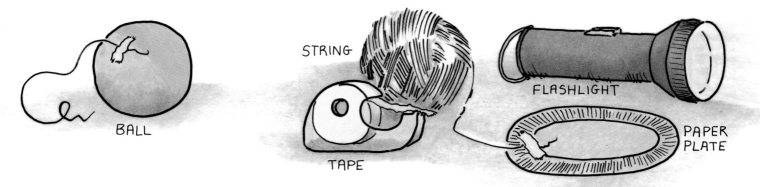

BALL

STRING

TAPE

FLASHLIGHT

PAPER PLATE

And that is how the Greeks found out the earth is round. You can test the discovery yourself. Shine a bright light on a plate, a can, and a ball. You can make each one cast a circle-shaped shadow on a wall in front of you. But only the ball always casts this shadow.

YARDSTICK

EMPTY CAN

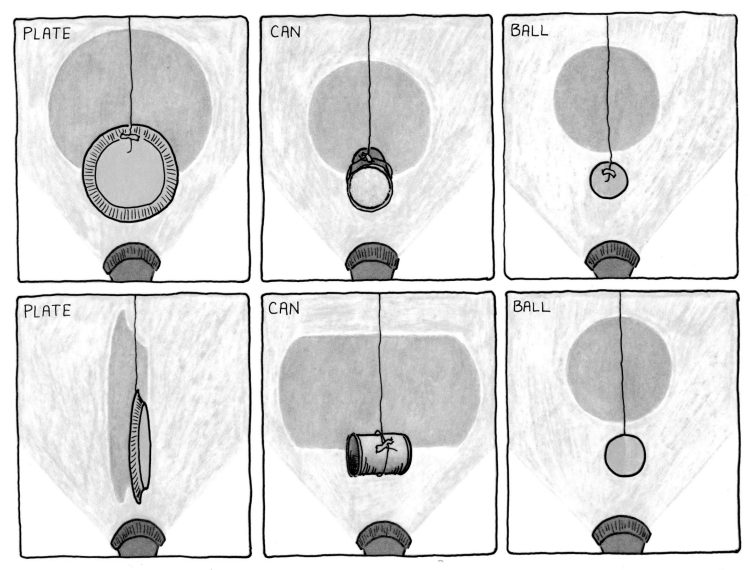

The Greeks made many other discoveries. One even worked out the size of the earth. He said it measured 25,000 miles around the middle. We know he was right, but some Greeks thought he was wrong.

These were Greeks who wrote geography books. They drew maps of the world as they knew it. They did not know about the Americas. So the maps showed Europe, Africa, Asia, and an ocean. This world did not look as if it could be 25,000 miles around. Geographers said it was smaller.

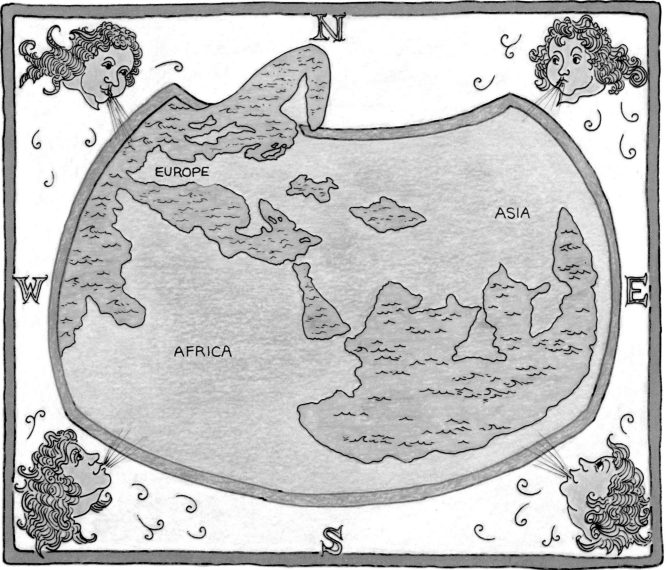

N

W   E

S

EUROPE

ASIA

AFRICA

19

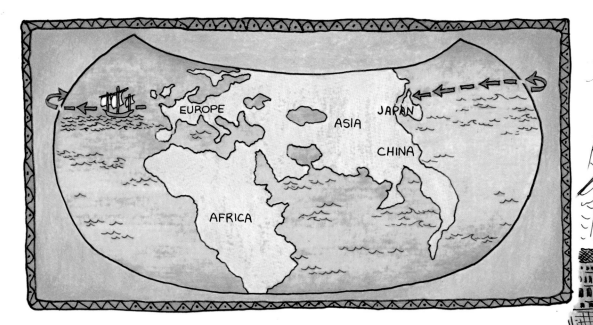

Early maps showed nothing but an ocean between Europe and Asia. If a ship sailed west, it should come to Japan and China. But ships were small. They could not carry much food or water, and maps showed nowhere to stop for supplies. No one set sail for Asia. No one needed to.

For hundreds of years traders carried goods overland from Asia to Europe. But during the 1400s, wars broke out and land routes were closed. Now people wanted to find a sea route to the lands of silks and spices they called the Indies—to India, China, Japan, and the Spice Islands.

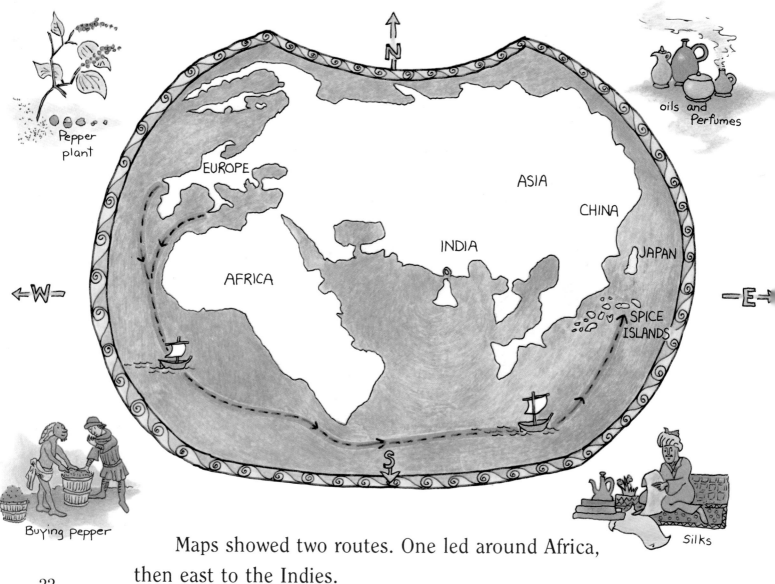

Pepper
plant

oils and
Perfumes

N

EUROPE

ASIA

CHINA

AFRICA

INDIA

JAPAN

W

E

SPICE
ISLANDS

S

Buying pepper

Silks

Maps showed two routes. One led around Africa,
then east to the Indies.

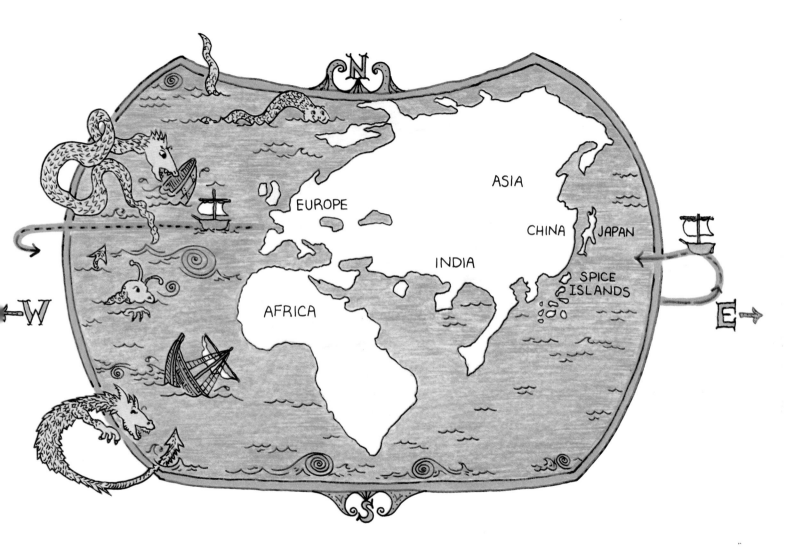

The other led west, across the unknown ocean.

Christopher Columbus wanted to sail west to the Indies. He read what the Greek geographers had said. He studied maps. The ones he liked best showed the ocean as quite small. The Indies seemed to be only a few thousand miles away. Columbus felt sure he could reach them.

On his first trip, Columbus found land just where
he expected to. He thought it was the Indies, but it
was not.

Columbus never reached the Indies. Other explorers soon discovered why. Columbus had reached a place that did not appear on their maps. He had reached a new world, which was later named the Americas. Beyond the Americas was another ocean, which must surely lead to the Indies.

EUROPE

ASIA

COLUMBUS
LANDS
HERE

INDIA

THE
AMERICAS

AFRICA

SPICE
ISLANDS

Ferdinand Magellan also believed the earth was smaller than it really is. He planned to sail around it—to find a way past the Americas and across the second ocean to the Indies. Then he would sail home around Africa.

It was a terrible trip that lasted three years. Many men lost their lives. One of them was Magellan. But when the survivors reached home, they had proved that the earth was really round and that ships could sail around it.

Today we have spaceships and
satellites in space. They take photos
of the earth. People everywhere
can see for themselves:

The earth is round.